CUTTING EDGE TECHNOLOGY

Cutting Edge Military Technology

ReferencePoint Press®

San Diego, CA

Other books in the Cutting Edge Technology set

Cutting Edge Military Technology

Barbara Sheen

San Diego, CA

© 2017 ReferencePoint Press, Inc.
Printed in the United States

For more information, contact:
ReferencePoint Press, Inc.
PO Box 27779
San Diego, CA 92198
www.ReferencePointPress.com

LIBRARY OF CONGRESS CATALOGING-IN-PUBLICATION DATA

Names: Sheen, Barbara, author.
Title: Cutting edge military technology / by Barbara Sheen.
Description: San Diego, CA : ReferencePoint Press, Inc., [2016] | Series: Cutting edge technology |
    Includes bibliographical references and index.
Identifiers: LCCN 2016006623 (print) | LCCN 2016006778 (ebook) | ISBN 9781682820445
    (hardback) | ISBN 9781682820452 (eBook)
Subjects: LCSH: United States--Armed Forces--Weapons systems--Juvenile literature. | Military
    weapons--Technological innovations--United States--Juvenile literature. | Military research--
    United States--Juvenile literature.
Classification: LCC UF503 .S53 2016 (print) | LCC UF503 (ebook) | DDC 623--dc23
LC record available at http://lccn.loc.gov/2016006623

Contents

Innovations in Military Technology

1813
Robert Fulton invents the first steam-powered armored warship; it carries thirty cannons.

1898
The USS *Holland*, the first practical submarine, is launched. It has an internal combustion engine for running on the water's surface and an electric motor for running underwater.

1951
In a test on an island in the Pacific Ocean, the United States detonates the first hydrogen bomb.

1800	1850	1900	1950

1860
The first repeating rifle, which allows marksmen to fire multiple shots without reloading, is manufactured by the Winchester Repeating Arms Company.

1945
The United States drops atomic bombs on Hiroshima and Nagasaki, leading to Japan's surrender and the end of World War II.

1958
Explorer I, the first US satellite, is launched—demonstrating US prowess in the space race against the former Soviet Union.

1955
The *Nautilus*, the first commissioned nuclear-powered submarine in the US fleet, is launched. Over the next few years, the submarine breaks all undersea vehicle distance and speed records.

2015
The US Army introduces Excalibur, one of the most powerful computers in the world. It improves the military's intelligence-gathering and communication capabilities.

1969
The earliest version of the Internet, known as ARPANET, is developed to protect the flow of information between military computers.

2010
Defense Department scientists use genetic engineering to create synthetic blood, thereby ensuring that military medics do not run out of blood for wounded troops.

1977
Work begins on development of the F-117 stealth fighter plane, the first aircraft designed around stealth technology.

1995
Abraham Karem designs the unmanned aerial vehicle Predator, launching a technological revolution in military aircraft.

1975   **1985**   **1995**   **2005**   **2015**

1983
The Humvee, a wide all-terrain vehicle designed to carry troops and cargo, is invented.

2011
The 40mm infrared illuminant cartridge, which enables troops to engage the enemy at night, is invented.

1973
To overcome problems caused by earlier navigation systems, the Department of Defense and three scientists begin work on a Global Positioning System.

2008
The heliplane, a combination of a helicopter and an airplane, is designed for use in military search-and-rescue missions.

New Technology to Meet New Challenges

The year is 2020. A naval warship detects an enemy cruise missile about 100 miles (161 km) away. The missile must be destroyed before it can reach its target. That is the job of a new weapon known as a railgun. Using electromagnetic energy, the railgun shoots out a missile-like projectile that travels at seven times the speed of sound. The projectile does not contain explosives. It uses kinetic energy—energy derived from motion—to do its job. This is how it works: The gun contains two parallel rails and a block of metal with the projectile on its tip, which travels along the rails. When a strong electric current is sent down the rails, it speeds the block of metal to the gun's barrel, where the projectile is released. It zooms out of the gun with such force that, upon impact, it produces 23.6 million foot-pounds of force, or 32 megajoules. To put this in perspective, 1 megajoule of force can move a 1-ton (.9 metric ton) object at a speed of 100 mph (161 km/h).

Not only is the gun powerful, but it also is cost effective. Whereas traditional missiles cost about $1 million apiece, railgun projectiles cost about $25,000 each. And they are lightweight. Ships that can carry only a few heavy missiles can hold hundreds of projectiles, making running out of ammunition unlikely. As Rear Admiral Matthew Klunder, the chief of US naval research, explained to Reuters news agency,

> Your magazine never runs out, you just keep shooting, and that's compelling. . . . We're also talking about a gun that's going to shoot a projectile that's about one one-hundredth of the cost of an existing missile system today. That . . . will give our adversaries a huge moment of pause to go: "Do I even want to go engage a naval ship?" You could throw anything at us, frankly, and the fact that we now can shoot

a number of these rounds at a very affordable cost, it's my opinion that they don't win.[1]

A History of Technological Innovations

The US Navy is currently testing railguns and plans to arm ships with them by 2020. Railguns are just one of a wide range of cutting edge technology under development by the military. From the earliest beginnings of the Internet to the development of global positioning system (GPS) and stealth technology, US military scientists, along with private companies, academics, and individuals working with the military, have always been in the forefront of new technological advancements.

The military has one goal: to protect the nation's security from real and potential threats. To do so, it must stay a step ahead of those who want to harm the United States. Throughout history, the military has worked hard to meet this goal by coming up with, improving upon, and/or adopting technological advancements that revolutionized warfare and were cutting edge for their

Soldiers in the US Army prepare an unmanned drone aircraft for flight. Drones can fly over vast regions for lengthy periods of time, sending camera images that military strategists use to pinpoint enemy activity or assess enemy defensive strength.

time. For example, the military is responsible for the adoption and refinement of the Gatling gun (the first rapid-fire gun and early forerunner of the machine gun), which gave the North a big advantage over the South in the Civil War. As a Northern soldier wrote in a letter home, "I think the Johnnys [Confederate soldiers] are getting rattled; they are afraid of our repeating rifles. They say we are not fair, that we have guns that we load up on Sunday and shoot all the rest of the week."[2] Similarly, the two-way radio, another military innovation, was essential to the winning of World War I. It allowed troops to send and receive messages over a distance, rather than depending on signaling with lights or flags or telegraph messages. New types of aircraft and the atomic bomb led to an Allied victory in World War II, and the development of unmanned aerial vehicles (UAVs) was essential to the US mission in Afghanistan, which began in 2001.

Changing Times and Changing Technology

Some early technological advances are still in use, but others have been replaced with newer technology. As times change, so does the way wars are conducted. Technology that gave the United States an advantage over its adversaries in the past may not be as useful in a different kind of war. Before the September 11, 2001, terror attacks on the United States, warfare resembled a chess game. Massive forces faced each other on battlefields using traditional tools of war such as guns and tanks. Manned aircraft loaded with bombs struck targets such as weapons arsenals, troop encampments, and weapons factories from a distance. For the most part, adversaries followed set rules of war. That changed when terrorists crashed two hijacked airplanes into the World Trade Center in New York City and one into the Pentagon in Washington, DC. (A fourth plane, intended for the White House, was diverted by passengers and crashed in a Pennsylvania field.)

insurgent

A nonmilitary person who fights against a country, government, or other formal authority.

Since then, the United States has been involved in asymmetrical warfare—warfare against terrorists and insurgents who avoid traditional military confrontations. Instead, these enemies employ unorthodox methods of warfare that do not follow any rules. They can strike anywhere, at any time, including attacking large population, cultural, and political centers. Targeting unarmed civilians, whether through physical attacks or through cyberattacks, is the norm for terrorists. Retaliating is not easy. Terrorists and insurgents are scattered all over the world. They often hide among civilians in populated towns, villages, and urban areas. They rarely wear uniforms. Likewise, many are quite willing to perform suicide missions.

Asymmetrical warfare requires new technology. In order to locate and track such elusive enemies, state-of-the-art surveillance and reconnaissance technology, including drones, robots, and cyber-spyware, is required. Once the enemy is located, weapons that can be delivered over long distances with great speed are needed. These weapons must be able to home in on targets with pinpoint precision to avoid collateral damage. Cyberweapons that can attack the enemy's vulnerabilities are also essential.

> **reconnaissance**
>
> **An exploratory military mission aimed at gaining information about an enemy.**

The US military is working hard to meet these challenges. It is developing all sorts of cutting edge technology to ensure our nation's security and preserve America's dominance in the changing face of warfare.

CHAPTER ONE

Robots to the Rescue

Almost everyone has seen a movie or played a video game in which robot warriors battle against each other. Although such scenes are fictional, the idea of substituting robots for human troops is currently in the works. Robots can be deployed faster than soldiers; they do not require food, training, or a paycheck. They can traverse difficult terrain, and they can go on missions that are too dangerous for humans. For these reasons, the US Army hopes to replace one-quarter of all brigade combat troops with robots by 2030. Indeed, robots are already playing a bigger role in warfare than ever before. In 2004 the military deployed a total of 163 robotic systems to Afghanistan and Iraq. By 2015 more than 7,000 were deployed overseas. According to General Robert Cone, head of the US Army's Training and Doctrine Command, the goal is to make the army "a smaller, more lethal, deployable and agile force."[3] To meet this goal, the Defense Advanced Research Projects Agency (DARPA), an agency involved in the development of new military technology, is working with a number of private companies on a variety of robots.

Doing Risky Work

Robots are machines that are programmed to perform a range of complex actions automatically. They are controlled in whole or in part by a computer, are capable of some form of locomotion, and have sensors that allow them to obtain information from their surroundings. Robots come in many forms. Typically, their shape and size are determined by their function. Unlike humans, robots cannot be killed. This makes them an excellent substitute for soldiers charged with high-risk missions such as locating and disposing of improvised explosive devices (IEDs).

IEDs are homemade bombs commonly used in asymmetrical warfare. They are a favorite weapon of insurgents and terrorists, who plant them along roadsides; under parked cars and bridges;

or in fields, caves, and alleys. They also conceal them inside abandoned buildings, in animal carcasses, and in rubbish. When IEDs are triggered, they send shrapnel in all directions, posing a serious threat to civilians and to troops. In fact, IEDs caused more deaths among NATO troops during the war in Afghanistan than any other weapon.

IEDs are diverse in design, are triggered in many different ways, and can be quite volatile. All of these factors make locating and disarming them treacherous. Robots designed to perform this job are helping to lessen the risk. The PackBot is one of these robots. A small robot operated via radio waves, the PackBot is controlled by a human operator using a laptop computer and a joystick controller. The PackBot weighs about 40 pounds (18 kg), so it is light enough for ground troops to carry in their backpacks. It moves on tank-like tracks with a rotating flipper on each end. The flippers allow the robot to negotiate stairs, climb over rubble and debris, and right itself if it gets turned over. The PackBot is also quite sturdy. In tests, it was able to survive a 6.5-foot (2 m) drop onto concrete without being damaged.

> **deploy**
>
> **To move troops and equipment into combat positions.**

There are multiple versions of the PackBot. Each is equipped with different payloads suitable for specific missions. The Fido version, which is inspired by bomb-sniffing dogs, possesses a special sensor capable of detecting vapors emanating from IEDs, along with a disrupter device that can disarm an IED. Other features include multiple cameras; a rotating wide-view video camera "head" that transmits real-time video and three-dimensional color graphics to the operator; and a long, maneuverable mechanical arm that can get into hard-to-reach areas and has grippers that can lift objects. The arm allows the robot to position the IED detection sensor close to suspicious objects. If the sensor detects an IED, a signal is sent to the PackBot's operator, who signals the robot to disarm or detonate the explosive. In this manner, the robot helps keep soldiers and civilians out of harm's way. As one marine staff sergeant explains,

As opposed to the other robots, it's a little smaller, but it's also quicker and more versatile and it has good line of sight and it could do a lot of stuff for us remotely so we don't have to—it can go out there and put itself in the line of danger. . . . Several cameras all around giving us a 360 [degree view] . . . on the front, back, and also on the arms so we can look at the gripper as well to make sure we know what we are picking up.[4]

Since 2002 about four thousand PackBots have been deployed to hotspots in the Middle East, and new, improved versions of the robot are in development. Although it is unknown how many lives the robot has saved, the number is certainly significant. As marine master sergeant Ted Bogosh, the manager of a joint robotics repair facility, explains, "Every day, we're getting robots that are blown up in some manner. Sometimes, it's something minor; sometimes they are actually dismantled. The explosion and the shrapnel may have disabled the robot, but they would have killed a person."[5]

Little Bots Doing Big Jobs

Military reconnaissance is another job for robots. Sneaking into enemy territory to learn what an adversary is up to is risky business. Increasingly, this work is being taken over by small robot spies. One of these is the Ember. A tiny version of the PackBot, the Ember weighs less than 1 pound (.45 kg) and can fit easily in a soldier's pocket. Like the PackBot, it moves on tracks and has two flippers. The Ember has a tiny camera mounted on one side. When troops want to survey a suspicious building without the risk of coming under fire, they toss in an Ember. The robot's camera relays whatever it sees in a live feed to a computer monitored by a human operator who controls the robot in much the same way as a PackBot is controlled. If

shrapnel

Metal pieces of a bomb, IED, or other explosive that fly outward from an explosion.

The PackBot

The PackBot is a small robot designed to fit into a standard US Army backpack. In Iraq and Afghanistan, PackBots have been used to clear caves and bunkers, search buildings, and defeat IEDs. The lightweight robot is designed to withstand rough treatment. Soldiers often toss it through windows, for instance, so that it can search for hidden enemy combatants. The PackBot is equipped with cameras, a maneuverable arm, and other devices. It relays real-time audio, video, and other data so that soldiers can see and hear what is taking place while remaining at a safe distance. Using treaded flippers, it can climb over obstacles and right itself if it lands upside down.

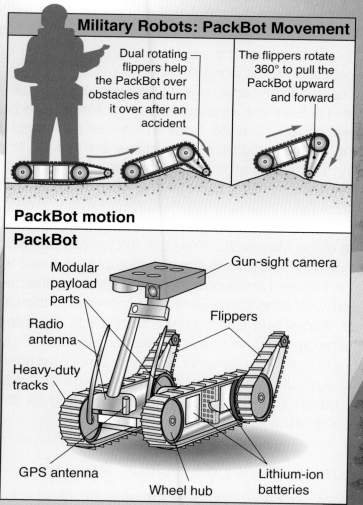

Military Robots: PackBot Movement

Dual rotating flippers help the PackBot over obstacles and turn it over after an accident

The flippers rotate 360° to pull the PackBot upward and forward

PackBot motion

PackBot

Modular payload parts

Gun-sight camera

Radio antenna

Flippers

Heavy-duty tracks

GPS antenna

Wheel hub

Lithium-ion batteries

Source: HowStuffWorks, "How Military Robots Work." http://science.howstuffworks.com/military -robot3.htm; Space Foundation, "iRobot PackBot Tactical Mobile Robot." www.spacefoundation.org.

a large area must be surveyed, large groups of Embers can be used simultaneously. The information they gather is networked and sent to one operator.

Other spy robots in development are even smaller than the Ember. One of the teeniest is the Meshworm, which is modeled after an earthworm and is about the size of an adult fingertip. It has a flexible, segmented body made of soft, springy, mesh-like material, which allows it to contort itself to squeeze into tight spaces. The Meshworm moves by stretching and contracting each segment of its body much like a real worm. The tiny robot is powered by electricity. It has wires, a miniature battery, and a circuit board inside it. When an electrical current is sent along the wires, the heat causes the wires to contract and then expand, which inches the robot along.

The size and soft nature of the Meshworm's body makes it an excellent spy. It is silent, inconspicuous, and almost indestructible. The miniature robot can be dropped from an airplane or thrown over long distances without being damaged. In fact, to test its durability, researchers stomped on the tiny robot and beat it with a hammer. Despite minor damage, the robot remained functional. According to Sangbae Kim, a professor of mechanical engineering at the Massachusetts Institute of Technology and one of the developers of the Meshworm, "You can throw [the Meshworm] and it won't collapse. Parts in Meshworms are all fibrous and flexible."[6]

The completed version of the Meshworm is expected to be equipped with sensors allowing it to gather and transmit temperature, audio, and video data to troops that are miles away. The Meshworm may also have medical applications for both the military and civilians. It, or other soft robots modeled after it, may be used in place of an endoscope, a hoselike medical instrument that is snaked through the body to examine internal structures such as the intestinal tract.

Mechanical Mules and Other Animals

Modeling a robot like the Meshworm after an animal is known as biomimicry. Biomimicry was also involved in the development of

DARPA

DARPA, which stands for the Defense Advanced Research Projects Agency, is an agency of the US Department of Defense dedicated to devising and developing new technologies for military use. DARPA was started in 1958 by President Dwight D. Eisenhower in response to the former Soviet Union's development of *Sputnik*, the first artificial Earth satellite. The agency has an annual budget of about $3 billion. It works with military scientists and engineers, private companies, universities, and individual researchers in the development of new technology.

DARPA has a number of divisions, each of which focuses on different types of technology and issues. Some departments focus on robotics and artificial intelligence; others focus on weapons and weapons delivery systems. Information technology is another area of concentration, as is biological and medical technology and communication technology.

To protect national security, many of the agency's projects are classified. Some past projects that have been revealed include the development of ARPANET, the earliest predecessor of the Internet; the Aspen Movie Map, a virtual-reality map that was a forerunner of Google Maps and Street View; night-vision goggles; and the computer mouse. The digital assistant, a forerunner of Siri, the iPhone's voice-recognition system, also began with DARPA. Still other DARPA technologies include cloud computing, driverless vehicles, and digital libraries.

the BigDog robot and the Legged Squad Support System (LS3, or AlphaDog), four-legged robots inspired by pack animals. When the terrain is too rough for wheeled or tracked vehicles, it is common for dismounted troops to carry 100 pounds (45 kg) or more of gear on their backs. This is hard work and often leads to back injuries. In fact, according to DARPA, "The Army has identified physical overburden as one of its top five science and technology challenges."[7]

The BigDog and the LS3 are designed to help relieve troops by carrying heavy loads over all sorts of terrain. Their legs, which are jointed like those of a real animal, allow the robots to jump

over obstacles, crouch down, balance on slippery surfaces, and move easily over rough terrain and steep inclines that wheeled or tracked vehicles cannot manage. "Most of the earth is inaccessible to vehicles, wheeled or track," says Marc Raibert, the president of Boston Dynamics, DARPA's partner in developing the LS3, "but the animal kingdom can go anywhere with legs. So the idea is to go anywhere animals can go."[8]

Both robots are powered by small engines working with a hydraulic pump. BigDog, which is the earliest version of the robot, is about the size of a large dog or a small mule. It weighs about 240 pounds (109 kg) and can carry up to 340 pounds (154 kg) of cargo. The LS3 is a super-sized version of the BigDog. It weighs about 800 pounds (363 kg) and can carry up to 400 pounds (181 kg) for 20 miles (32 km) without refueling. Both robots are equipped with a spinning camera mounted where an animal's head would be and a computer system with sensors that direct the positioning of the robots' leg joints, the force of each step, and when and how each leg makes contact with the ground. This keeps the robots from losing their balance. Onboard communication and vision sensors make it possible for the robots to follow troops carrying an electrical device in their backpacks.

As a newer, more technologically advanced version of the Big-Dog, the LS3 is capable of navigating via GPS. The LS3 also has visual and hearing sensors that make it possible for it to respond to hand gestures and voice commands like "follow," "stop," and "stay." The goal is for the robot to interact with troops in much the same way as a trained animal and its handler interact. Moreover, the LS3 can do something that a real animal cannot do: troops can use the robot to charge their cell phones and other handheld devices.

To keep the LS3 from being damaged during combat, a bulletproof version is currently in the works. Both robots have passed field tests and have successfully participated in military games. The Big-Dog is currently training with US Marines on their base in Quantico, Virginia. It

hydraulic

A term used to describe a system or tool moved or operated by fluid.

should not be long before both robots are embedded with soldiers and marines on ground missions.

Another animallike robot, known as the WildCat or the M3 (Maximum Mobility and Manipulation), may be joining the Big-Dog and the LS3. The WildCat is another four-legged robot very similar in appearance to the BigDog. It is powered by a go-kart engine working with a hydraulic pump. Whereas the BigDog is relatively slow moving, the WildCat is built for speed. Modeled after a cheetah, the robot can sprint and gallop at 16 miles per hour (26 km/h), but the goal is to improve its speed to 50 miles per hour (80 km/h) on all kinds of terrain. To put this in perspective, humans run at an average of about 5 miles per hour (8 km/h).

Much like an actual cheetah, the WildCat has a jointed back and jointed legs that flex on each step, increasing its stride and running

The WildCat animallike robot has jointed legs for striding. The WildCat was modeled after the cheetah (pictured), a cat that can reach speeds up to 74 miles per hour. Currently, the WildCat can only gallop at 16 miles per hour, but engineers hope to improve that speed in the future.

speed. Even at high speeds, it is quite agile and stable. Like its other four-legged counterparts, it will be equipped with cameras, communication equipment, and sensors. Although DARPA has not said in what type of missions the robot will be used, one possible use would be speeding supplies to frontline troops.

Future Bots

Other robots are being designed to move on two legs like humans. One interesting DARPA project is named after the movie *Avatar*. In that movie, humans were hooked up to a brain interface pod that allowed them to control giant genetically engineered human-alien hybrids. The idea for the pod has its basis in telepresence technology. Telepresence is a relatively new set of technologies that allow people to feel as if they are present, or appear to be present, at a distant location, as in teleconferencing and virtual-reality simulations. It also allows a human operator to affect what is happening at a distant location via a brain-actuated robot.

The aim of the Avatar project is to use telepresence technology in the development of a lifelike two-legged robot that would substitute for human troops on the field of battle. The robot would be capable of performing combat duties such as sentry duty, combat casualty recovery, room clearing, and battlefield missions, keeping its human counterpart out of harm's way. It would be controlled by a soldier miles away via brain-computer interface technology. This new type of technology uses thoughts in the form of brain waves to communicate with and control machines. According to DARPA, "The Avatar program will develop interfaces and algorithms [mathematical formulas that a computer can follow] to enable a soldier to effectively partner with a semi-autonomous bi-pedal machine and allow it to act as the soldier's surrogate."[9]

Other than that statement, DARPA has not revealed how the technology will work. If it is anything like existing brain-computer interface programs, a human operator will wear a headset with a set of electrodes that attach to the operator's scalp and wirelessly connect to a computer. The electrodes are part of an electroencephalograph (EEG), a device that measures and records the different electrical signals produced by the brain whenever a person thinks, moves, feels, or remembers something. The signals are streamed to the computer, where special software converts them into algorithms. The algorithms are sent via the Internet to the robot, which is programmed with software that converts the algorithms into actions that the robot will perform.

algorithm

A set of instructions, in the form of numbers, for a computer to follow.

Brain-computer interface technology is still in an early stage of development, and the Avatar program presents a lot of challenges. First of all, coming up with algorithms for all the activities and thoughts that are necessary in battle is a tremendous task requiring the work of gifted mathematicians, computer scientists, and brain scientists. Secondly, EEG equipment is bulky and not as effective as implanting electrodes directly into a person's brain. And finally, depending on the Internet as a connection between the soldier and the surrogate raises the risk of cybercrime. Moreover, delays on the Internet are common.

A Robot Jellyfish

Researchers at Virginia Tech are working with the US Navy to develop a self-powering robot that looks like a giant jellyfish. The robot is named Cyro after the *Cyanea capillata* jellyfish, and its design relies on biomimicry. A jellyfish moves through water by contracting and relaxing muscles in its bell-shaped body. As the muscles contract, they enclose water in the jellyfish's body. When the muscles relax, the water is expelled, which propels the jellyfish along. As Virginia Tech doctoral student and researcher Alex Villanueva explains, "We are trying to get it as close as possible to the natural animal. The way it looks, the way it moves, the general feel of it."

Cyro has eight aluminum arms and a flexible silicone covering. It is about 67 inches (170 cm) long and weighs 170 pounds (77 kg). A built-in, preprogrammed controller allows the robot to act autonomously. When it is finalized, it will be used for underwater surveillance missions.

Researchers are working on a way to power Cyro so that it can stay in the water for months at a time. They are experimenting with a variety of alternative energy sources, including solar power and wave energy. Another possibility is for the robot to supply its own energy through a chemical reaction between the oxygen and hydrogen in seawater, or through fuel cells powered by bacteria found in ocean waters.

Quoted in Natalie Angley, "Robotic Jellyfish Could Be Undersea Spy," CNN, May 8, 2013. www.cnn.com.

Nevertheless, DARPA has allotted $7 million to fund the program. Based on the agency's history as a technology innovator, it is likely that it will succeed. In fact, it has already been successful in using brain-computer interface technology in experiments with monkeys. In one program, a monkey implanted with a computer chip in its brain moved a robotic arm—which was not connected to the monkey in any way—with its thoughts. It may be three or more decades before robot surrogates replace human warriors. But if things go well, someday what we now think of as scenes on a movie screen may be the new face of warfare.

CHAPTER TWO

Unmanned Aerial and Marine Vehicles

In October 2015 two US air strikes over Afghanistan's Nazyan district by unmanned aerial vehicles (also known as UAVs or drones) destroyed a terrorist compound, killing nineteen Islamic State, or ISIS, militants and wounding three others. These air strikes were just two of many similar missions. UAVs are an essential part of the US war on terrorism, and for good reason. UAVs are less costly to operate than manned aircraft, and they minimize the risk to US forces. In addition, they can hover over an area until they identify the perfect target, the perfect time to strike, and the best location from which to drop their payload. This makes it possible for drones to deliver weapons with almost pinpoint precision, resulting in fewer civilian casualties and less collateral damage than other methods—an important asset when it comes to asymmetrical warfare.

In fact, according to New America, a think tank based in Washington, DC, during the administration of President Barack Obama, drone strikes killed an estimated thirty-three hundred terrorists associated with organizations including al Qaeda, ISIS, and the Taliban. UAVs hurt terrorists in other ways too. Because UAVs are equipped with sensors that detect on-the-ground electronic equipment, to avoid detection terrorists must often rely on human runners to deliver messages. Since runners can be captured or killed, messages do not always get through. UAVs also make training groups of new recruits problematic for terrorists. The aircraft carry state-of-the-art cameras that can easily spot suspicious gatherings. And many carry weapons that can destroy training camps. Not surprisingly, an instructional sheet found among terrorist belongings in Mali directed fighters to "maintain complete silence of all wireless contacts [and] avoid gathering in open areas."[10]

UAVs are such a critical part of the war on terror that, as of

2016, the aircraft made up one-third of the US Air Force's fleet. The military relies on UAVs to execute combat and noncombat missions, and it is continually developing new technology to make these vehicles more versatile.

Eyes in the Sky

UAVs are robotic aircraft. They come in many sizes and shapes. Some have a wingspan of more than 100 feet (30 m), but others are so small that they look like flying insects. As the name implies, unmanned aerial vehicles do not need a pilot inside them to fly. Most are semiautonomous. They are remotely operated by pilots who may be near the target zone or thousands of miles away on the ground, in a control center, or on a ship at sea. Using a computer and a joystick, drone pilots send commands to the aircraft by means of a satellite link. The drone transmits information back to the pilot in the same way. Some UAVs operate completely autonomously, without any help from a distant pilot. They carry out preprogrammed missions under the control of an onboard computer using GPS coordinates.

UAVs are capable of performing a variety of military missions, including reconnaissance, surveillance, and weapons delivery. They can be equipped with bombs and missiles, video and still cameras, listening devices, radar, and sensors designed to detect chemical and biological weapons, among other gear. Some UAVs are powered by batteries and propellers. Others have jet engines that allow them to fly more than 500 miles per hour (805 km/h) and climb upward of 50,000 feet (15,240 m). These capabilities enhance their ability to scan large distances. In addition, most drones do not need to be refueled as often as manned aircraft, nor do they have to land in order to relieve exhausted crew members. As a result, many UAVs can stay in the air for twenty-four hours or more, providing uninterrupted reconnaissance and surveillance. They can also fly into hostile areas that may be too risky for manned aircraft to enter.

autonomous

Able to act without outside control.

An army captain controls a drone from a base in the Kandahar region of Afghanistan. Using a joystick and computer, the "pilot" can maneuver the distant aircraft to perform surveillance or even drop ordnance or fire off missiles.

Predator and Global Hawk

Two of the best-known military drones are the Predator and the Global Hawk. The Predator entered military service in 1995. It has been deployed in Europe, Africa, the Middle East, and Asia. The earliest versions were used for reconnaissance and surveillance missions. After the September 11, 2001, terrorist attacks on the United States, the aircraft was redesigned to carry and fire precision-guided weapons such as the laser-guided Hellfire missile. This required new engineering—for instance, the wings had to be reinforced so that the aircraft could withstand the force of launching a missile, and specially designed mounting brackets to hold the missiles had to be added.

Armed Predators have been used by both the military and the CIA to hunt

radar

A system that sends out radio waves that are reflected back to the sender in order to determine the speed or location of a moving object.

Flybot: A Tiny Drone

Scientists at Harvard University, in conjunction with DARPA, are developing a tiny UAV known as the Flybot that resembles a flying insect. Small enough to fit on an adult's fingertip, the Flybot is made of lightweight carbon and weighs less than a pin. Like most drones, it is controlled by a pilot from a distance. The military plans to use Flybots for reconnaissance missions in areas too dangerous for humans, including places contaminated by chemical or biological weapons.

The Flybot's size and appearance make it hard to detect, especially if it can be maneuvered into a swarm of real insects, where it can hide in plain sight. The drone is equipped with a tiny microprocessor, sensors, and a transmitter. Researchers hope to power the drone either with solar or nuclear energy.

Scientists came up with the idea for the minute flyer while researching how to create a birdlike UAV that could flap its wings, making it hard to distinguish it from an actual bird. Such a drone has not yet been developed, but work on the Flybot is ongoing.

down and kill terrorist leaders. One of the drone's earliest successes occurred in 2009, when a Predator took real-time video of Taliban leader Baitullah Mehsud on a rooftop patio of a house in northwest Pakistan. The video was streamed to a pilot on the ground, who remotely launched two Hellfire missiles from the aircraft, killing Mehsud and eleven of his followers. Upon reviewing the video, Pakistan's interior minister, A. Rehman Malik, said, "It was a perfect picture. We used to see James Bond movies where he talked into his shoe or his watch. We thought it was a fairy tale. But this was fact!"[11]

As of 2015 there were more than seven thousand Predators in the US arsenal. In that year alone, Predators flew an estimated thirty missions per day over Syria and Iraq in the war against ISIS. Newer, more cutting edge versions of the aircraft are constantly being developed. The most recently updated, bigger version is known as the Reaper. Whereas the Predator is about 27 feet (8 m) long and has a wingspan of about 48 feet (15 m), the Reaper is about 66 feet long (20 m) and has a wingspan of about 36 feet (11 m). Because it is larger, it can carry a larger payload. Like the Predator, the Reaper can stay in the air for twenty-four hours. But it can operate at higher altitudes—about 50,000 feet (15,240 m), which is almost double the Predator's maximum ceiling.

Other new features include synthetic aperture radar (SAR). SAR is an airborne radar imaging system that is used to generate high-resolution two- and three-dimensional images of scenes on the ground. SAR uses the motion of the aircraft to create a simulated antenna or aperture in place of a large antenna. To create an image, radio waves are sent from the drone to the ground. The echo of each wave is reflected back to the drone, where it is recorded. As the drone moves, so does the SAR system relative to the target. The multiple images are combined to form high-resolution images that without SAR technology would be impossible to capture without a football-field size antenna. The images are so clear that it is possible for the drone to make out tiny details like footprints.

The Predator and its successors are probably the best-known military UAVs. But there are many others, such as the Global Hawk, which is equipped like the Predator and the Reaper. However, it is almost double the length of the Reaper, can reach an altitude of 60,000 feet (18,288 m), and can stay in the air for thirty-two hours.

Another drone, known as the RQ-180, is in development. It is modeled after the Global Hawk, with a very important new feature: stealth technology. Stealth technology uses special materials that make an aircraft undetectable by radar. This makes it possible for the aircraft to slip into hostile territory without being discovered. In addition to stealth technology, the RQ-180 is equipped with electronic and radar surveillance equipment. Although the RQ-180 will be used mainly for surveillance and reconnaissance, it has electronic warfare capabilities that will enable it to disrupt electromagnetic equipment such as computers, cell phones, and electronically controlled weapons delivery systems used by the enemy.

The MQ-9 Reaper is larger than its predecessor, the MQ-1 Predator, and can carry a larger payload. The Reaper can hold and launch antitank or antipersonnel munitions such as Hellfire missiles or the Paveway II guided bomb.

UAV Swarms

Currently, most UAVs operate as solo vehicles. In contrast, manned fighter jets operate as a squadron. If things go as planned, small, semiautonomous UAVs operating as a swarm may eventually be integrated with, or even replace, manned fighter jet squads. In nature, a swarm is a group of animals that move in concert and communicate with each other to complete tasks. An example is a flock of birds that take off at the same time and fly in precise formation, seeming to move as one entity. The birds coordinate their movements with that of their closest flight neighbors. So when one bird changes speed or direction, so do the other birds in the vicinity.

A drone swarm operates in a similar manner. One drone, programmed with a flight plan, is designated the swarm leader. The other swarm members are programmed to follow the leader. The leader signals its position and speed several times per second to sensors on the other aircraft. The sensors relay this information to an onboard autopilot that adjusts the vehicle's speed and direction accordingly. Other sensors ensure that each aircraft maintains a safe distance from the next by taking continuous measurements of each aircraft's position in relation to each other and signaling changes when needed. In this manner, the swarm maintains formation, which is not an easy task. Vijay Kumar, a University of Pennsylvania robotic engineer and project researcher, explains:

> What a robot [UAV] has to do is determine where its neighbors are and figure out what the relative position is and then monitor the relative separation very carefully. You only need to tell one robot [the designated leader] how to move, and the other robots essentially maintain formation, by just keeping a specified relative distance. In the figure eight they come within inches of each other, so they have to combat aerodynamic effects from their neighbors, and they have to have very, very precise control.[12]

Each drone is about 4 feet (1 m) long. Their small size makes it possible to launch them from ships, tactical vehicles, or aircraft, out of tubes that catapult the UAVs into the air in rapid succession. Every member of the swarm can be equipped differently, making it possible for a single swarm to complete multiple missions. For instance, one swarm member can be equipped with surveillance cameras while another can carry sensors that detect chemical or biological weapons. Others can carry different munitions, including, if all goes as planned, laser weapons. The military hopes to put UAV swarms into operation in the near future.

Swarming Unmanned Boats

The US Navy is taking the swarm concept from air to sea. In October 2000 the navy destroyer *Cole* was docked in Yemen for refueling. Terrorists in a small boat slipped up beside the destroyer and detonated explosives, killing seventeen sailors and wounding thirty-nine others. In an effort to prevent such an attack from happening again, the navy is developing swarms of self-guided unmanned patrol boats to escort and protect large ships.

Like UAV swarms, the unmanned boats (known as unmanned surface vehicles or USVs) move and act in concert and are programmed to react to a number of possible scenarios. For example, in a typical mission a swarm of USVs would float around

Stealth Technology

Researchers are working on developing stealth drones. In nonstealth aircraft, radar signals sent from the ground reflect off the aircraft back to the ground station, which lets the enemy know the location of the aircraft. Nonstealth aircraft are rounded, which makes them aerodynamic. Their rounded form, however, makes it possible for radar signals to hit almost anywhere on the aircraft and be reflected back to the sender.

Stealth aircraft are designed to be almost invisible to radar. They have flat surfaces and sharp edges that reflect radar signals at different angles, making it unlikely that the signals will reflect back to the enemy. In addition, stealth aircraft are covered with special paint that absorbs radar signals. As a result, stealth aircraft are very hard to detect.

The RQ-170 Sentinel is a stealth drone that is operational. It is V-shaped, resembling a flying wing. Although much of the information about the Sentinel is classified, the stealth UAV has been reported to have been used for reconnaissance and surveillance missions over Afghanistan, Pakistan, and Iran. In 2011 a Sentinel aircraft was reportedly captured by Iran. The Iranian media reported that the nation's electronic warfare division had hacked into the drone's electronic communication signal, commandeering the UAV. Photos of the vehicle appeared in Iranian media. It is not known whether the event was fabricated or actually occurred. If the Sentinel was captured, it is likely that the technology will be sold to enemies of the United States.

a warship. If its sensors detected a suspicious boat approaching, the swarm would break free of the ship and encircle the craft, keeping it away from the warship. If the craft refused to stand down, the USVs could fire on it. However, to prevent the boats from mistakenly firing on an innocent craft, firing control would come from a sailor on the warship monitoring the swarm.

In other scenarios, USV swarms could be used by the US Coast Guard to protect American harbors. The boats would swarm on enemy boats and ships entering the harbor. Sam

Calabrese, a US naval officer who piloted an "enemy" vessel in a field test of the swarming boats, says, "If I was the actual target it would be pretty intimidating to see five boats rushing at me."[13]

Each USV is controlled by a sensor and software kit that was originally designed by NASA for the Mars rovers and was adapted by the navy for use on small boats. Known as Control Architecture for Robotic Agent Command and Sensing (CARACaS), the kit can be fitted onto almost any small boat, making it possible to turn currently manned patrol boats into USVs that can operate as part of a swarm.

Swarming USVs are expected to be in operation shortly. They will free up sailors who otherwise would be deployed on manned patrol boats, and they will help protect sailors and marines on warships. As Rear Admiral Matthew Klunder, chief of naval research, explains, "While the attack on Cole was not the only motivation for developing autonomous swarm capability, it certainly is front and center in our minds. . . . If Cole had been supported by autonomous USVs, they could have stopped that attack long before it got close to our brave men and women on board."[14]

Unmanned Submarines

The navy is also involved in developing unmanned underwater vehicles (UUVs). Designed to perform surveillance, underwater mine detection, harbor blockades, and antisubmarine warfare, UUVs help keep sailors and marines out of harm's way by taking over some of the riskiest missions. For example, underwater mines pose a hazard for ships and submarines. Typically, the navy uses dolphins to find and mark mines in coastal and inland waterways. Once this is done, human divers lay charges around the mines to detonate them. In deeper water, the navy relies on ships and helicopters towing submerged sleds equipped with sonar to locate mines. Both scenarios put sailors in danger. Divers must swim away before the mines explode, ships must navigate mine-infested waters, and low-flying helicopters are easy targets for enemy marksmen. In contrast, UUVs take humans out of the equation.

UUVs come in many sizes and shapes. One of the most cutting edge is an autonomous unmanned submarine known as the Manta. The craft has a teardrop shape, much like a manta ray fish. In fact, when it moves underwater it can easily be mistaken for a fish. Its shape and quietness allows it to hover near the seafloor unnoticed.

The Manta is about 100 feet (30 m) in length. Each Manta can carry four cruise missiles or torpedoes as well as swarm-size UUVs or UAVs, making it possible for a Manta to release swarms and weapons. Future manned submarines are being designed with a special docking area large enough to hold four Manta craft. While a Manta is docked, its weapons are operational. This means the weapons can be discharged from the mother ship without launching the drone, just like any weapons the ship carries.

Once a Manta is launched, it uses onboard sensors, a powerful sonar system, and a high-tech steering system to navigate autonomously. Some sensors let the UUV locate chemicals that underwater mines emit, and others reveal changes in the local magnetic field caused by metallic objects such as mines, missiles, and torpedoes. The UUV is covered with smart skin—special fabric that acts as armor for the craft. The smart skin contains electronic sensors that can set off an electrical charge capable of disabling incoming missiles. If a Manta identifies an enemy threat that requires it to release its payload, it communicates with the mother ship via computer. The UUV cannot discharge munitions without permission from a human operator on the mother ship. Once its mission is complete, the Manta returns to the mother ship and redocks itself.

The harshness of an underwater environment makes developing unmanned underwater vehicles like the Manta a challenge. Visibility is limited underwater, and currents and waves can throw a vehicle off course. GPS and radar do not penetrate deep water, complicating navigation and communication. "Everything's

sonar

A device or system that sends out sound waves that are reflected back to the sender in order to detect and locate objects underwater.

For decades, the navy has employed dolphins with cameras to nimbly swim through mine fields and spot these hidden explosives. More recently, unmanned underwater vehicles have taken over this dangerous task to spare injury to the dolphins and human divers.

working against you underwater,"[15] says Robert Wernli of the Ocean Systems Division of the Space and Naval Warfare Systems Center. In field tests, however, the Manta appears to have overcome these challenges, and it should be operational soon.

Indeed, unmanned vehicles are becoming a key part of the military's arsenal. In the not-too-distant future, drones of all kinds will take over the missions of many manned crafts, keeping troops safer. "Every so often in history, there's a tech that comes along that rewrites the rules of the game," P.W. Singer, a fellow at the Brookings Institution, says of drone technology. "I describe this as a revolution."[16]

CHAPTER THREE

State-of-the-Art Weapons

Having superior weapons gives warriors an advantage over their adversaries. To get this advantage, the military is continuously developing new weapons. And because the nature of warfare is changeable, these weapons are designed to fit the different faces of war.

High-Speed Weapons

On August 20, 1998, in retaliation for terrorist attacks on US embassies in Africa, President Bill Clinton ordered warships in the Arabian Sea to fire cruise missiles at an al Qaeda training camp in Afghanistan. Intelligence placed terrorist leader Osama bin Laden at the camp, which was located more than 1,000 miles (1,609 km) away from the launch point. It took almost two hours for the missiles to reach the target. Although several militants were killed in the attack, Bin Laden had left the camp shortly before the missiles hit. If the missiles had been capable of striking at greater speed, it is likely that Bin Laden would have been killed in the air strike, and the September 11, 2001, terrorist attacks against the United States might not have occurred. To take better advantage of this type of opportunity in the future, the military is developing a variety of high-speed weapons.

Hypersonic missiles are one of these weapons. To be classified as hypersonic, a missile or aircraft must be capable of traveling at a minimum of Mach 5 (five times the speed of sound) or 3,800 miles per hour (6,116 km/h). To put that speed in perspective, if a hypersonic missile had been available in 1998, it could have reached the al Qaeda camp in about twelve minutes. What is more, such weapons are so fast that they are able to avoid being detected by radar or other early warning systems.

The development of hypersonic weapons is part of the military's Prompt Global Strike Program. The goal of the program is to come up with a method of delivering nonnuclear weapons any-where on Earth in under an hour. Hypersonic technology, however, is complex, so this a challenging task. The military has looked at a number of approaches. One of the simplest is to use existing inter-continental ballistic missiles (ICBMs) as a delivery system. ICBMs are three-stage rockets capable of traveling at speeds reportedly greater than 13,400 miles per hour (21,600 km/h). ICBMs are usually armed with nuclear warheads, which would not be difficult to replace with conventional warheads that could be delivered at hypersonic speed. As a matter of fact, China successfully tested an ICBM loaded with conventional warheads in 2014. However, because other nations might assume that an ICBM flying over their airspace is the start of a nuclear attack and retaliate in kind, this option could prove to be dangerous.

Another possibility is using a scramjet as a weapon delivery system. A scramjet is an airplane designed to fly at rocket speed. However, scramjet technology is still in its early development, and there is one big problem involving the use of an internal combus-tion engine at hypersonic speeds. Jet aircraft take in oxygen from the atmosphere and use it to ignite fuel in an internal combus-tion engine. Air entering a jet engine at speeds beyond Mach 3 causes the engine's movable parts to melt and the airplane to disintegrate.

A NASA B-52 takes off with a Pegasus rocket under its wing. At the tip of the rocket is an X-43 Scramjet set up for a test flight. The unmanned scramjet can reach speeds of up to 6,600 miles per hour (10,600 km/h). However, such high speeds can cause the aircraft to malfunction and even disintegrate.

Scramjet technology seeks to solve this problem by using a jet engine without moving parts. In a scramjet, the aircraft takes in air at supersonic speeds and compresses it until it is blisteringly hot. When this air mixes with jet fuel, it produces massive thrust, which allows the aircraft to travel at Mach 5 or above. The engineering involved is extremely delicate. The high speed of the incoming air requires the air and fuel to mix and burn in a very short time. And keeping the combustion rate steady at such speeds is tricky. The burn rate is hard to control, and until the technology is perfected, there is always a danger of the aircraft exploding. The military has talented engineers working on these issues. If all goes well, it hopes to be able to use scramjets to deliver hypersonic missiles by 2020.

Supercavitating Torpedoes

Other superfast weapons are being developed for underwater missions in the form of supercavitating torpedoes. Currently, torpedoes launched from submarines can travel at about 50 miles per hour (80 km/h) and have a range of only a few thousand feet. The drag from the water a torpedo travels through slows its movement and can cause it to sink. A supercavitating torpedo does not have this problem. It is launched from a rocket engine on a submarine. Upon its launch, a nozzle on the torpedo's tip releases gas that envelops the torpedo, creating an almost frictionless bubble around the weapon. The gas bubble allows the water to flow around the torpedo without creating drag and slowing its movement. Although supercavitating torpedoes do not travel at hypersonic speeds, the navy has tested one that broke the sound barrier and exceeded Mach 1.

drag

When air or water pushes back on an object as the object moves through it, slowing the object's speed.

Supercavitating torpedoes are not ready for combat missions. Several challenges remain. For example, if the torpedo changes direction, the bubble no longer fully envelops the weapon. Kam

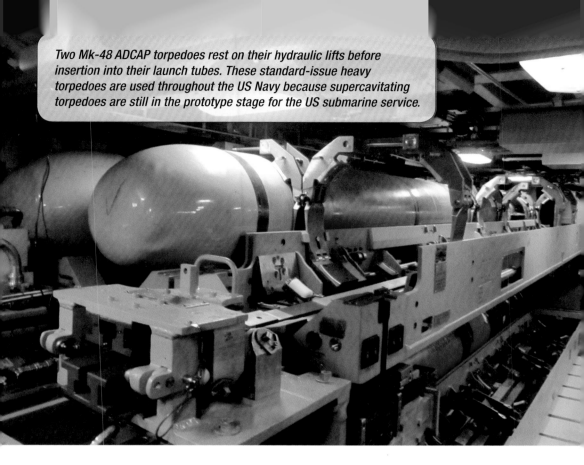

Two Mk-48 ADCAP torpedoes rest on their hydraulic lifts before insertion into their launch tubes. These standard-issue heavy torpedoes are used throughout the US Navy because supercavitating torpedoes are still in the prototype stage for the US submarine service.

Ng of the US Navy's Office of Naval Research explains: "If your torpedo moves in a straight line, you just aim and shoot. That capability already exists. . . . When you turn, the gas bubble distorts because it is no longer symmetrical. So you have to compensate for that by putting more bubble to one side."[17] Researchers theorize that this can be done by ejecting more gas toward the outside of the turn, and they are working on perfecting the weapon. The torpedoes are expected to be ready for combat by 2020.

Laser Weapons

Other new weapons seem to be taken straight from the movies. Almost everyone has seen cinematic space travelers draw laser ray guns and, with a rapid flash of light, destroy enemy targets. Although ray guns are not yet in development, other laser weapons are no longer fictional.

The word *laser* stands for "light amplification by stimulated emission of radiation." A laser is a device that produces a very powerful, focused beam of light via a chemical or electrical reaction. Laser light is different from regular light. Regular light travels in different directions and wavelengths; therefore, it spreads out and loses intensity as it travels. A laser beam, on the other hand, moves in one direction and has all the same wavelength. As a result, it does not spread out or lose intensity as it travels. This enables a laser beam to maintain a precise course even when traveling long distances.

Laser beams produce intense heat and strike with great speed and precision. Used as a weapon, a laser can burn a hole through an aircraft, intercept and destroy a rocket or a surface-to-air missile, or explode a concrete bunker, among other possible missions. As Peter Morrison of the Office of Naval Research explains, "The future is here. The . . . laser is a big step forward to revolutionizing modern warfare with directed energy, just as gunpowder did in the era of knives and swords."[18]

The military has a number of programs aimed at developing laser weaponry. In 2014 the US Air Force tested the High Energy Laser Mobile Demonstrator (HEL MD), a laser weapon designed to locate, track, attack, and destroy drones, missiles, rockets,

mortar

A weapon that fires explosive projectiles.

and mortars. Mortars especially are a big problem in battlefield situations. Current technology detects incoming mortars and sets off an alarm, warning troops to take cover. However, current technology does not have the capability to accurately destroy incoming mortars. With the HEL MD, mortars can be destroyed before they hit, protecting human lives. In fact, as part of the 2014 test, the HEL MD successfully shot down more than 150 flying targets, including drones, and more than 90 mortar rounds. A video of the test showed the HEL MD accurately targeting and hitting the mortars, causing them to burn up in midair before finishing their flight path or detonating.

As its name implies, the HEL MD is a mobile weapon that can be mounted on a large truck and taken right onto the battlefield.

Nonlethal Weapons

In cases of civil unrest or humanitarian missions, military personnel charged with keeping the peace often face violent crowds. To control such situations, the military relies on nonlethal weapons.

Nonlethal weapons are weapons that are less likely to cause death than traditional weapons. A Taser, for example, sends electric shocks carried by fine wires to a person's body, temporarily incapacitating him or her. Other cutting edge electrical weapons, such as electric bullets, are in development. Electric bullets can be fired from a gun or grenade launcher. When the bullets hit a person, they deliver a powerful but nonlethal electric shock.

Another nonlethal weapon known as a directed stick radiator uses electricity to deliver painful sound waves. An electrical signal is fired through a tube that contains a series of electrical discs. As the signal passes through the first disc, a loud noise and a burst of energy is produced. The noise and energy level is repeatedly magnified as the signal passes from disc to disc. The result is a sound level and shock wave that causes disabling pain.

Another weapon uses microwaves to produce painful sound. If microwaves are exposed to pulses of low energy, a strong sound sensation is produced in a target's head. The military is working on delivering microwaves via rifle-like guns or through large systems that could disperse big crowds.

The missile is equipped with a special telescope and infrared cameras for locating and selecting targets. The HEL MD's laser is powered by lithium ion batteries, which are charged by a diesel generator carried on the truck. As long as the generator has fuel, the HEL MD can fire indefinitely.

It takes two people to operate the HEL MD. One drives the truck, and the other controls the weapon using a laptop computer and a handheld controller. The military plans to use the HEL MD as an alternative to more expensive traditional weapons in the near future.

When the HEL MD is deployed it will join another laser weapon known as LaWS (Laser Weapons System). LaWS was deployed in 2014 on the USS *Ponce*, a naval transport ship serving in the Middle East. LaWS operates much like the HEL MD, but it is smaller in size and strength. It is constructed to be mounted on a ship, where it can be used to shoot down small drones and disable small boats. This makes LaWS a good weapon for use in the Persian Gulf, where small, fast boats commanded by hostile forces harass US ships.

infrared

Invisible electromagnetic radiation that is emitted by heat and has a wavelength just less than that of the red end of the visible light spectrum.

Like the HEL MD, LaWS is powered by electricity, which makes it a lot safer than carrying traditional explosives on a ship. It is also much more economical to operate than standard weapons. Other laser weapons designed for use in marine combat are also in the works. As a 2013 report issued by the Congressional Research Center explained,

Compared to existing ship self-defense systems, such as missiles and guns, lasers could provide Navy surface ships with a more cost effective means of countering certain . . . targets. [Laser weapons] could lead to changes in naval tactics, ship design and procurement plans for ship-based weapons, bringing about a technological shift for the Navy—a "game changer"—comparable to the advent of shipboard missiles in the 1950s.[19]

Space Weapons

Ground, sea, and air weapons are not the only weaponry used by the military. The military relies on satellites in space for communication, navigation, and intelligence gathering. In fact, in 2003 US and British cruise missiles attacked warships in the Persian Gulf in a surprise attack that signaled the start of the Iraq War. The missiles were guided by GPS from satellites thousands of miles overhead.

NAVSTAR military satellites regularly orbit the earth, giving ground, air, and sea forces accurate images of geographic locations as well as the positioning of friendly and enemy units. They are also used to provide direction signals to smart weapons aimed at enemy targets.

Satellites can be natural or artificial objects that orbit a planet. The moon is an example of a natural satellite. The International Space Station is an example of an artificial satellite. Artificial satellites act like giant mirrors; radio signals sent from transmitters on Earth reflect off a satellite in an uplink and bounce back to receivers elsewhere on Earth in a downlink. Software in the receiver converts the signals into data, sounds, and/or images. Satellites have many different purposes. Communication satellites, for example, allow people all over the world to communicate via telephone and the Internet. Television satellites bounce television programs

From Theory to Application: Newton's Law of Gravitation

When military scientists plan on putting a satellite into orbit, they rely on Isaac Newton's law of gravitation to ensure that the satellite will not collide with other satellites. The law of gravitation states that any two objects, no matter their mass, exert gravitational pull or force on each other. The force varies depending on the exact mass of each object and the distance between them. Using a mathematical equation, scientists can figure out how much force two satellites exert on each other and the best location for a new satellite.

from one part of the world to another. Navigation satellites provide GPS, and other satellites are used for weather forecasting, gathering information, and scientific studies, among other things.

As of 2016 approximately three thousand satellites orbited Earth. About one thousand belong to the United States, and many of these are operated by the US military. Navigation Signal Timing and Ranging (NAVSTAR) GPS is an example of a group of more than two dozen military satellites working in concert to continuously transmit navigation signals to receivers on Earth. The signals are incredibly accurate, giving the military almost all the information it needs to determine the location of troops, equipment, and enemy forces on the ground, in the air, and at sea. Weapons like cruise missiles and smart bombs rely on the signals to pinpoint their targets. Manned and unmanned aircraft, marine vehicles, and ground troops also use satellite signals for navigation. Indeed, satellites are so vital to US security that an attack on US military satellites could disable the armed forces' ability to navigate, communicate, or gather intelligence effectively, and an attack on US civilian satellites could disrupt telecommunications and transportation systems.

A nuclear weapon could destroy a satellite in low orbit. During the Cold War, both the United States and the Soviet Union explored this option. But the possibility that such a blast could spread radioactive fallout back down to Earth led to the passage of the Outer Space Treaty of 1967, which banned the use of nuclear weapons in space. Other nonnuclear weapons, however, known as antisatellite (ASAT) missiles, have been developed and tested. In a 2014 test, China successfully used an ASAT to destroy one of its own weather satellites. Six years earlier, the United States shot down a malfunctioning reconnaissance satellite using a modified ASAT.

ASATs are launched from an F-15 fighter jet. The jet climbs rapidly, then releases an ASAT that uses preprogrammed navigational directions to home in on the designated target. However, when an ASAT hits its target, the explosion can send a large amount of debris into orbit indefinitely. Orbital space debris moves at extremely high speed, making it very destructive if it collides with a satellite or a manned spacecraft. Says author Bruce W. MacDonald, "One only has to imagine what life would be like if thousands of bullets from World War II were still whizzing around to get some feel for the danger that debris growth poses for the future of space."[20]

Like MacDonald, many people feel that it is in the world's best interest to prevent a buildup of space debris. In fact, a number of nations, including the United States, have agreed to nonbinding regulations aimed at minimizing the growth of space debris. Consequently, the military is investigating alternatives to ASAT missiles, including using laser weapons to disable but not destroy enemy satellites.

Hypervelocity Rods

Other nonnuclear space weapons being studied would not be fired at a satellite but instead would be fired from an orbiting satellite down to targets on Earth. An example is hypervelocity rod bundles. This weapon, which is also known as Rods from God, uses kinetic energy, or energy derived from motion, to produce the destructive power of a nuclear weapon without any radioactive fallout. Two satellites working in tandem with a ground operator are needed to operate the weapon. One satellite serves as a communication platform for the weapon. The other is armed with the weapon, which consists of a bundle of large, thin tungsten rods, each measuring about 20 feet (6 m) in length and 1 foot (30 cm) in diameter. Upon instructions from the ground, the targeting satellite signals the other satellite to fire the rods, which, depending on the mission, could be fired either singularly or en masse at targets on Earth. To ensure their accuracy, the rods could be fitted with imaging sensors and a navigational guidance system. And since tungsten is a hard metal that can withstand extreme heat, the weapon does not need heat shields to survive the heat of reentering Earth's atmosphere.

tungsten

A hard metal with a very high melting point (6,170°F/3,410°C).

The rods essentially act like meteors. They pick up speed as they fall to Earth, reaching about 8,000 miles per hour (13,000 km/h) by the time they reach their target. Due to this speed, the weapon would be difficult to defend against, and the force of its impact could cause considerable damage. Since the bulk of the force would be directed downward, it could penetrate deep underground bunkers that terrorists use as a defense against enemy aircraft and destroy underground installations where rogue nations purportedly shelter nuclear weapons.

Information about hypervelocity rod bundles is limited due to military secrecy. It is unknown whether the weapon is in development or is simply a concept at the present time. But since the US military's space budget amounts to more than $7 billion per year, and maintaining the nation's space superiority is essential to national security, it is likely that along with high-speed and laser weapons, cutting edge space weapons will be part of future warfare.

Ready for Action

The year is 2025. American soldiers climb over rooftops searching for hostile insurgents. The soldiers look like futuristic ninjas. They are dressed in form-fitting, multifunctional suits that change color, serve as body armor, and enhance strength and endurance, among other features. Their motorcycle-style helmets are equipped with microprocessors, cameras, microphones, and a visor-mounted display. Although the soldiers look as if they have stepped out of a science fiction movie, scientists are currently developing this type of tactical gear. Their work began in the 1990s with a project known as the US Army's Land Warrior system and goes on today with the Future Warrior 2025 and Future Warrior 2030 programs. The combined goal is the creation of tactical gear that will protect soldiers while boosting their battlefield awareness and combat capabilities. As author Kevin Bonsor explains, "As warfare changes, armies are looking for any advantage they can get against potential enemies. The new . . . suit will take human performance to unprecedented levels. Imagine a platoon of soldiers wearing suits that turn an ordinary person into a real live superhero."[21]

The Suit

The Future Warrior uniform uses new and developing technology to create a unique garment. The suit, which is still in development, has three layers and is powered by electricity. The layer closest to the body contains microprocessors that channel electricity through the suit, allowing the suit to serve as a data "taxi" that carries information from one part of the wearer's body to another. Microturbines fueled by liquid hydrogen supply electricity for three days. To extend the energy supply, soldiers carry cartridges with extra liquid hydrogen, which provide them with enough power for a total of six days in the field.

The microprocessors have many other functions. An important

one is tracking the wearer's vital signs. Data related to the wearer's health, such as blood pressure, heart rate, and temperature, is continuously transmitted to medics and commanding officers who may be miles away. A computer that sits on the base of the soldier's back and connects to local and wide-area wireless networks serves as a transmitter. Soldiers can access their own health data through a voice-activated drop-down display inside their helmets.

This system allows commanding officers to monitor the well-being of combat troops. It also makes it possible for medics to tell if a warrior is in need of health care, no matter his or her location. Even from a distance help is available. For example, if a soldier is suffering from dehydration, information detailing the soldier's condition will be transmitted to a medic. The medic then sends a message to a microprocessor embedded in the soldier's helmet, advising the soldier to drink water. The message immediately appears on the drop-down screen inside the soldier's helmet. Upon seeing the message, the soldier sips from a tube inside the helmet that is connected to a water pack carried on the soldier's back.

microprocessor

A silicon chip that contains all of the functions of a computer's central processor on a single, integrated circuit.

Medics can also observe a soldier's body temperature. If the temperature is elevated, the medic can send a signal to a 5-pound (2.27 kg) microclimate-controlling system that soldiers wear on their hips. Upon receiving the signal, the system sends cooling fluid through slender tubes that run through the suit. Conversely, if a soldier is too cold, the device sends heated fluid through the uniform. Additionally, if the medic determines that the soldier needs hands-on medical attention, a message, map, and directions that guide the soldier to the nearest medical professional appear on the drop-down screen.

Nanotechnology in Action

Besides monitoring a soldier's health, the suit has other state-of-the-art functions. The middle and top layers of the suit provide

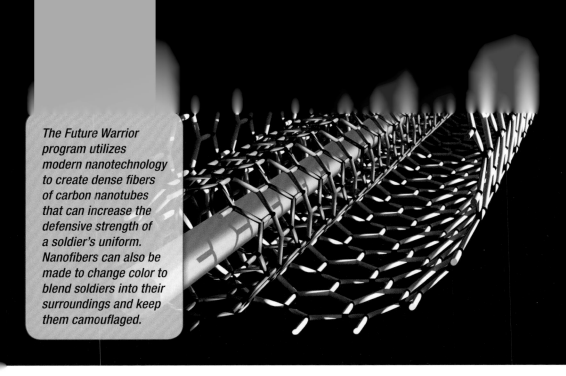

The Future Warrior program utilizes modern nanotechnology to create dense fibers of carbon nanotubes that can increase the defensive strength of a soldier's uniform. Nanofibers can also be made to change color to blend soldiers into their surroundings and keep them camouflaged.

soldiers with body armor and camouflage. To do so, the suit relies on nanotechnology. Nanotechnology involves the manipulation of atoms and molecules to create miniscule fibers, particles, devices, or systems about fifty thousand times smaller than the diameter of a human hair. Nanotechnology is so important to the development of new tactical gear that in 2012 the army funded a $50 million nanotechnology research program, known as the Institute for Soldier Nanotechnologies, at the Massachusetts Institute of Technology. According to army specialist Jean-Louis DeGay of the Soldier System Center, a military research center, "If we were in Detroit, the . . . Future Warrior system would be the concept car. It leverages a lot of the nano-work being done by the Massachusetts Institute for Technology."[22]

In the case of the Future Warrior suit, nanoparticles further enhance the suit's capabilities. Nanoparticles can increase a fabric's strength, chemical resistance, and antibacterial properties and can conduct electricity, among other applications. For the future soldier uniform, nanoparticles are being developed that respond to light by changing color to reflect the wearer's surroundings. This would make soldiers almost undetectable. As former air force chief of staff General John Jumper explains, "We must give the individual soldier the same capabilities of stealth and standoff that fighter planes have."[23]

Other nanofibers in development protect soldiers from harmful chemicals. When woven into the suit, these fibers block chemical toxins from penetrating the wearer's skin or internal organs. At the same time, fire-retardant nanoparticles make the suit nonflammable. Nanoparticles with antimicrobial properties are also in the works. Troops in combat get very dirty. By keeping dirt and bacteria away from the skin, suits with antibacterial nanoparticles will reduce the incidence of skin irritations and fungal growth that often plague soldiers in the field. Nanofibers that resist fleas, ticks, and other insects are also being researched for inclusion in the suit.

Nanotechnology may also improve the strength of the suit while acting as body armor. At present, combat soldiers wear body armor made out of Kevlar, a specialized fiber that is woven into bulletproof vests. However, Kevlar is heavy and can slow a person down. Moreover, it can absorb only a limited number of strikes. More effective lightweight liquid body armor is being developed to replace Kevlar. It is composed of magnetorheological fluids—nanoparticles of iron suspended in oil. When an electric current is applied to the fluid, the nanoparticles lock onto each other and the fluid becomes stiff, causing bullets to bounce off the rigid shield.

magnetorheological

A substance whose properties are modified by a magnetic field.

The plan is to place magnetorheological fluids throughout the middle and top layers of the Future Warrior uniform. Sensors programmed to recognize a ballistic threat will transmit an electric current to the fluid when it is needed. When the threat is gone, the flow of electricity is stopped, the particles unlock, and the substance becomes soft liquid again. "We're salivating like Pavlov's dogs about this one," says DeGay about the liquid armor.

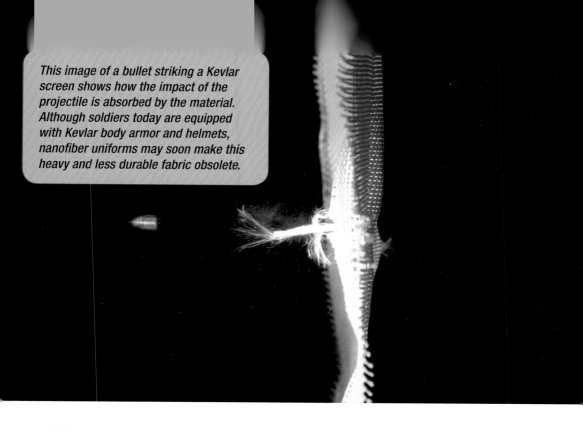

This image of a bullet striking a Kevlar screen shows how the impact of the projectile is absorbed by the material. Although soldiers today are equipped with Kevlar body armor and helmets, nanofiber uniforms may soon make this heavy and less durable fabric obsolete.

"We're talking about head-to-toe body armor which weighs only 16–18 lbs. [7–8 kg] and can be worn all the time. It will give complete protection instead of just covering the vital organs."[24] At the same time, the liquid armor will be able to absorb repeated strikes without cracking as Kevlar sometimes does. "When you have a uniform with this new nanotechnology, it can absorb unlimited numbers of machine-gun rounds,"[25] DeGay explains.

Researchers also hope to use the liquid armor fluid to help injured troops. If a soldier breaks a bone, for example, a steady electrical pulse could be sent to the liquid around the bone. This would cause the liquid to harden, creating a temporary cast.

The Helmet

The helmet too has multiple functions. In fact, it serves as the uniform's command central. It is embedded with sensors and microprocessors that control and coordinate all of the systems and functions related to the headgear. These include communication,

From Theory to Application: Pascal's Law

Hydraulics are used to power many military devices, including robotic exoskeletons currently in development. The science behind hydraulics is based on work by the French mathematician Blaise Pascal and is known as Pascal's law. The law states that when there is a change in pressure or force at any point on static fluid in a closed system, the change in force will be equal on the fluid in every other part of the closed system. The closed system can be a single container, or it can be a complex system connected by hoses or pipes. So, for example, in a simple hydraulic system that consists of two pistons and a pipe filled with oil that connects them, when pressure is applied to one piston, the force is transmitted to the other piston through the oil in the hose.

voice translations, hearing, and situational awareness systems. The helmet also provides troops with night vision and voice-activated weapons control. In addition, it contains a GPS and radio receiver, and local and wide-area Internet connections, allowing for rapid data transfer.

The helmet looks like a futuristic motorcycle helmet. But it does a lot more than protect the wearer's head. Its visor contains a 17-inch (43 cm) transparent drop-down display screen. Making the screen transparent allows wearers to use their eyes for other activities while looking at the screen. Soldiers can activate the screen with their voice without having to put down their weapons. Virtual-reality technology and a graphic computer interface let soldiers interact with photos, maps, and real-time videos projected onto the screen. Much like picture-within-a-picture television technology, the screen can break down at the wearer's command into multiple screens so that several images can be viewed and compared.

Microprocessors in the helmet arrange the pixels of these images so that they match the curvature of the visor, allowing soldiers to view the images from every angle. Such images may be sent to the soldier from headquarters, satellites, or reconnaissance aircraft. As DeGay explains, "If an Apache helicopter was deployed forward and recorded real-time video of the enemy, the helicopter can send the video back to an individual soldier to observe."[26] With virtual-reality technology, maps can also be projected onto the ground to give soldiers a larger view.

Besides receiving images, the helmet contains a built-in 360-degree camera that takes video and infrared images of everything around the wearer. These too are projected onto the screen, boosting the wearer's situational awareness. The images and video can also be streamed in real time to squad members or to the home base. This feature lets distant commanders see and hear everything soldiers see and hear. It also helps protect troops. For instance, if a soldier's headgear camera detects an IED, a photo of the explosive and a map of its location appear on that soldier's screen. The photo and map are also streamed to squad members, warning them to steer clear of the weapon. Soldiers can also chat with each other online via the local network or by voice-controlled text messages that appear on the recipient's screen. Messages from headquarters can also be sent in the same manner. This allows troops to stay in constant touch with each other and instantly be alerted to possible threats or sudden changes in orders.

In 2007 troops deployed in Iraq tested out an early version of the helmet as part of the army's Land Warrior (LW) project. Lieutenant Colonel Bill Prior, commander of an infantry battalion that used the LW helmet, was pleased with its capabilities. He had this to say about the technology: "LW is a leap ahead in solving the age-old problem of 'touch' [contact] between men and small units in the close fight. You are not alone even if you do not have voice or visual contact with other LWs."[27] In other words, even in the heat of battle when troops may not be able to easily see or speak to each other, the helmet allows them to stay connected.

Additional Enhancements

The helmet protects soldiers in other ways as well. It safeguards them from loud noises that can damage their hearing and amplifies soft sounds. A sensor in the headgear monitors environmental

Underwater Gear

The US Navy has developed a diving suit that allows divers to dive to a record depth of 2,000 feet (610 m). The suit, which is known as the Hardsuit 2000 or the Atmospheric Diving System, makes it possible for divers to rescue trapped submarine crews. "Its specific purpose," explains Commander Keith W. Lehnhardt, the officer in charge of the project, "is to be part of the advance assessment system during a submarine rescue operation. The diver in the suit will see what the damage to the sub is and find out where the survivors might be."

The suit took eleven years to develop and costs $2.7 million. It weighs 1,700 pounds (771 kg). Although it is quite bulky, it has side-mounted thrusters and footpads that enhance its maneuverability and make it easy to control direction. Oil-filled floating joints in the arms and legs give divers flexibility, and special hand pods allow divers to hold and use tools. The helmet contains a video camera that lets sailors on a nearby ship monitor the diver. It also contains sonar, which helps divers find hidden targets. To keep the diver from getting decompression sickness, which is caused by rapid changes in air pressure, the suit regulates atmospheric pressure.

In rescue missions, divers wearing the suit are attached to a frame that is lowered from a ship. When divers are within about 30 feet (9 m) of the stranded target, they unhook themselves from the frame and proceed with the mission.

Quoted in Mark G. Logico, "Navy Chief Submerges 2,000 Feet, Sets Record," America's Navy, August 4, 2006. www.navy.mil.

sounds by measuring sound vibrations in the soldier's skull. The sensor connects to software that automatically amplifies or lessens sound to a discernible and safe level. "What this will allow you to do is know where that sniper round or mortar round came from, but at the same time it will cancel out noise at a certain decibel so as not to cause damage to the soldier's ears,"[28] explains Sergeant Robert Atkinson, who is working on the project. This technology also allows troops to focus on the slightest sound and amplify it, making it easier to determine where the sound is coming from and whether it was made by a hidden adversary.

Other technology in development will potentially help soldiers involved in asymmetrical warfare identify adversaries dressed in civilian garb, a common practice among insurgents and terrorists. Integrating artificial intelligence software into the display will make it possible for soldiers to take a photo of a potential enemy and check it against biometric facial-recognition databases of known enemies in real time. Additionally, the image would be stored in the database for future reference, and troops would also be able to transmit the image and the biometric data to other soldiers.

A Robotic Exoskeleton

Another part of the Future Warrior uniform is a wearable robotic exoskeleton that gives an ordinary person super strength, speed, and endurance. Mimicking the exoskeletons depicted in movies like *Iron Man*, robotic exoskeletons are mechanical devices that come in different shapes and forms. One version in development consists of two powered mechanisms similar in appearance to leg braces. These run along the outside of a soldier's lower limbs and up the wearer's back, connecting to a computer in the soldier's backpack. The computer links to a hydraulic power system and to sensors in the exoskeleton. When the sensors detect contractions of the wearer's muscles, a signal is sent to the computer. It in turn

> **exoskeleton**
>
> **A robotic frame that serves as an external skeleton, enabling the wearer to move faster and carry a heavier load.**

signals motors known as actuators to deliver high-pressure hydraulic fluid to the exoskeleton's joints, which provides the power to assist movement of the limbs. The device also relies on gravity by shifting the weight of heavy loads to the ground.

Exoskeletons currently in development have enough power to work for a maximum of five hours. The biggest challenges researchers face is providing the exoskeleton with at least twenty-four hours of power without weighing it down. Current versions

The armored exoskeleton of the popular comic book and film character Iron Man may soon become a reality for future soldiers. As prototypes are perfected, the military expects such powered suits will give soldiers greater endurance, carrying capacity, and strength.

weigh about 53 pounds (24 kg) and are constructed of a combination of strong, lightweight, and flexible materials such as aluminum and titanium. To ensure the exoskeleton fits soldiers of different heights, its length varies.

The primary purpose of the exoskeleton is to enhance a soldier's strength. Unmounted combat troops currently carry gear that can weigh about 100 pounds (45 kg); likewise, logistic and support troops are estimated to lift, load, and unload about 16,000 pounds (7,260 kg) during a typical workday. Musculoskeletal injuries are therefore common among military personnel, but robotic exoskeletons will help protect troops from such injuries. In tests, wearers of the device can easily carry 200 pounds (91 kg) for extended periods without exhaustion or strain. This not only would make carrying heavy gear easier, but it also would make it possible for a small soldier to carry a larger injured squad member to safety. It would also let troops carry heavier and more powerful weapons. As David Audet, a researcher at the US Army Natick Soldier Research, Development, and Engineering Center, explains, "We're trying to augment the soldier, augment the marine, to be able to perform tasks that he does every day, safer, more efficiently, and trying to reduce the energy in those tasks and reduce that number of injuries."[29]

Power to the legs would also make it possible for soldiers to run greater distances and speeds with reduced fatigue. The latest versions allow wearers to run at about 10 miles per hour (16 km/h). Researchers hope to develop technology that will allow runners to reach even greater speeds and increase their ability to leap and jump higher. At present, exoskeleton wearers can squat, crawl, leap, and jump at normal levels with minimal exertion.

Robotic exoskeletons are not yet ready for current missions. If all goes well, however, soldiers will be wearing the devices along with the new uniform in the not-too-distant future. The cutting edge technology involved in the suit, helmet, and exoskeleton will potentially give American troops an advantage over enemies. At the same time, it will no doubt make soldiers' jobs easier and keep them safer.

CHAPTER FIVE

Cyberwarfare

Until recently, warfare has taken place within four domains: land, sea, air, and space. With the growth of information technology, a fifth domain—cyberspace—has been added. According to Major General Daniel O'Donohue, commander of Marine Forces Cyber Command, "Cyber is . . . just the same as air, sea and land. . . . If there is any question about this being a warfighting demand, you have to look at the enemy. . . . They believe our critical vulnerability is cyber, and they are coming at us every day for that potential contest."[30]

Almost everyone—governments, businesses, private citizens, and the military—has access to and relies on computers, electronic systems, and data networks for everything from telecommunications to missile defense. Attacks across cyberspace are a daily occurrence. Cyberattacks on the military can be used to gather information stored in computers. Or they can be used to disable, disrupt, or destroy computer-run military communications, GPS navigation, UAVs, weapons, and weapons-delivery systems. As Jarno Limnell, the director of cybersecurity at Stonesoft, a company that develops network security systems, explains,

> There is a world of bytes and a world of atoms, and increasingly the world of bytes is driving the world of atoms. . . . Almost all weapons systems today run on some kind of software. Missiles are very useful if you can launch them, if you can't launch them, they are useless.[31]

What makes cyberattacks especially alarming is that cyberwarfare includes, and even concentrates on, civilian targets. The world's financial institutions, electrical grids, telecommunication systems, and water treatment plants are all run by computers. Attacking such infrastructures can cause many problems for society. For instance, during the 2015 war between Russia and

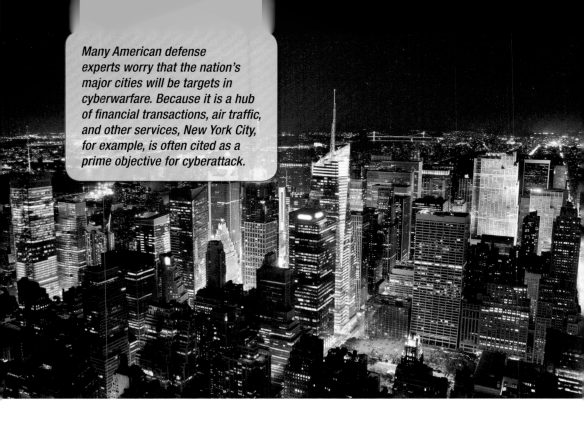

Many American defense experts worry that the nation's major cities will be targets in cyberwarfare. Because it is a hub of financial transactions, air traffic, and other services, New York City, for example, is often cited as a prime objective for cyberattack.

Ukraine, cyberattacks against Ukraine disabled civilian cell phone service and caused other difficulties as well.

Complicating matters further, cyberattacks can come from anywhere. Enemies are not separated by physical barriers but rather by electronic firewalls. Attacks can be committed by nations, rogue states, terrorists, and individual hackers. As a matter of fact, in 2015 ISIS supporters calling themselves the Cyber Caliphate took credit for hacking into the YouTube and Twitter accounts of the military's US Central Command. Although the hack did little damage, it showed that the group is capable of cyberterrorism. Indeed, in a video that was released shortly after the attack, an ISIS supporter threatened, "We are the hackers of the Islamic State. The electronic war has not yet begun. We observe all the movements you are making from your devices. Soon you will see how we control your electronic world."[32]

Moreover, unless cyberattackers take credit for their work, the anonymous nature of cyberspace can make identifying attackers and responding to attacks difficult. Although data sent

Electromagnetic Warfare

Electromagnetic warfare has been around since World War II. Because it and cyberwarfare share many similarities, the military often classifies them together. Electromagnetic warfare involves disrupting or destroying signals along the electromagnetic spectrum (ES). Any system, vehicle, weapon, or mission that involves infrared, radar, cellular, television, or radio waves is part of the electromagnetic spectrum. This includes remotely detonated bombs, drone signals, military guidance systems, and radio communications as well as civilian cell service and radio and TV.

Jamming radio signals is one way to attack an adversary's communications and radar systems. One way this is done is with aircraft that fly over enemy territory searching for radio signals. Once the signals are identified, special electronic equipment on the aircraft analyzes the signals and sends out other radio signals designed to jam the equipment. Electromagnetic equipment can also be destroyed with electronic bombs, or e-bombs. E-bombs work by producing a powerful electromagnetic pulse (EMP). When an EMP hits any type of electronic equipment, it sends a large electric current through the equipment, which destroys the electronics.

over the Internet includes information about the source, savvy hackers can make it seem like the attack is coming from a different, false source.

Undoubtedly, cyberwarfare presents many challenges. To meet these challenges and take advantage of opportunities to attack an enemy's computer systems, the military is ramping up the development of cutting edge technology aimed at making the United States the most cybercapable nation in the world. As James Lewis of the Center for Strategic and International Studies wrote in a 2015 report, "No modern military can expect to operate successfully without cyber capabilities for both defense and offense. Similarly, no country can perform its national security and public safety functions without adequate cyber capabilities."[33]

The Cyber Grand Challenge

According to the Techopedia website, the term *cyberattack* can be defined as "deliberate exploitation on computer systems, technology-dependent enterprises, and networks. Cyberattacks use malicious code to alter computer code, logic or data, resulting in disruptive consequences."[34]

There are different types of cyberattacks. Most involve malware, or software designed to perform unwanted actions to a computer system. Malware is frequently used to steal information, spy on a victim, or destroy something on a computer. Malware comes in different forms, including spyware, viruses, worms, and Trojan horses. Malware can enter a computer through the Internet or via an infected flash drive. Once malware gets into a computer, it attaches to computer programs and files and replicates. Some types of malware, like viruses, depend on human action to spread, but others, like worms, can spread from one operating system to another without human assistance.

Depending on its mission, malware can delete or damage files or cause individual computers, operating systems, or web and network servers to fail. Malware can also hide in a computer and gather information. Other forms of malware also exist, and people with malicious intent keep coming up with new ways to do damage. In fact, private companies that develop antivirus software report seeing huge numbers of new malware programs every day.

In an effort to counter existing and new cyberattack methods, DARPA is sponsoring a contest known as the 2016 Cyber Grand Challenge. The goal is to develop a computer system that can detect and defuse cyberattacks instantaneously without human assistance. Currently, cyberdefense relies on human experts to recognize and neutralize attacks and fix weaknesses in the system. Human experts also distribute corrective software to friendly systems, thereby inhibiting future attacks. This process takes time, however, and since malware can do lots of damage in a few hours, there is a need to speed up the process. As DARPA program manager Mike Walker explains, "The only effective approach to defending against today's ever-increasing volume and

Attacking a Computer's Guts

In 2015 the Kaspersky Lab, an international security firm, reported that US Cyber Command (representing all branches of the US military) had developed a new type of malware capable of attacking a computer's firmware. *Firmware* is a term used to describe a set of instructions that is permanently embedded in a computer's hardware. Firmware controls how a computer communicates with the other computer hardware. Such a weapon can keep an infected computer from booting up or operating correctly. It can also serve as an encryption-cracking tool, giving hackers the ability to identify the computer's encryption key and access confidential data without being detected.

It is very difficult to attack a computer's firmware, but the new malware appears to do just that. It is reported to burrow so deeply into computers that it cannot be detected or wiped out by antivirus programs. And because it attacks firmware rather than regular software, even if a computer's software is reinstalled, the malware can keep reinfecting the computer. Therefore, such a weapon could cause long-term, serious problems for an enemy.

diversity of attacks is to shift to fully automated systems capable of discovering and neutralizing attacks instantly."[35]

The 2016 Cyber Grand Challenge began in 2014 with more than 104 cybersecurity teams participating. The teams consisted of security industry professionals, engineers, computer scientists, academics, hackers, and other interested individuals from around the world. Based on their performance in qualifying events, the number of teams was gradually narrowed down to seven teams who will compete in the final challenge in August 2016. One of the latter qualifying events, known as Capture the Flag, consisted of a real-time computer security contest. But rather than hackers and computer security experts competing against each other to see who was the fastest at detecting and reversing malware, for the first time ever in any Capture-the-Flag contest, machines were the only players. Participating teams created computers with innovative self-defending systems and software designed to identify and reverse-engineer infected software that DARPA came up with for the contest. According to DARPA,

> The event operated at a speed and scale at which only machines can compete. . . . Most CTF [Capture the Flag] events challenge experts to analyze and secure about 10 pieces of software over 48 hours. The CGC [Cyber Grand Challenge] Qualifying Event demanded that teams' machines work on 131 pieces of [infected] software—more than any previous CTF event—over just 24 hours. Some teams' systems secured single pieces of software in less than an hour. . . . [The event] resulted in participating teams together fixing all of the 590 flaws in the competition software of which the contest developers were aware.[36]

The final challenge will consist of the same procedure; however, the malware will be even more complex and harder to detect. Teams will be scored on how quickly and effectively their computer systems identify a cyberattack, protect the hosts, and keep the hosts' software running without any problems. The top three teams will receive large cash prizes. More importantly, the event has already produced multiple approaches to improving cybersecurity. "We want an automation revolution in computer security so machines can discover, confirm and fix software flaws within seconds, instead of waiting up to a year under the current human-centric system," Walker says. "These capabilities are essential for protecting data and processes as more and more devices, including vehicles and homes, get networked."[37]

Plan X

The Cyber Grand Challenge is just one of many ways DARPA is trying to increase the military's cyberstrength. Since 2013 DARPA has been working on Plan X, a project that extends through 2017. It is aimed at developing new, easy-to-use technologies that will improve the military's ability to launch cyberattacks and defend against retaliation. Part of Plan X makes use of virtual-reality technology that enables cyberwarriors to feel as if they are inside the Internet. DARPA researchers think that the experience will help troops prepare for and better understand cyberattacks.

In tests, subjects wear a virtual-reality headset that interfaces with the wearer's brain. Each subject is assigned different missions involving offensive and defensive cybersecurity breaches. Each is also given a series of instructions about what actions must to be taken to successfully fulfill each mission and a set of virtual tools to use. Then the test subjects virtually enter the Internet. Here, immersed in a maze of coding, networks, subnetworks, and data, they face an attack by an enemy and must successfully counter with their own attack. DARPA researchers think this kind of three-dimensional visualization will give prospective cyberwarriors a stronger sense of how the Internet works and how to detect and neutralize malicious actions. It will also help them better understand how to identify a target's weaknesses and how best to take advantage of such weaknesses. As DARPA's Plan X program manager, Frank Pound, explains, "You're not in a two-dimensional view, so you can look around the data. You look to your left, look to your right, and see different subnets of information. . . . With the Oculus [the virtual-reality headset] you have that immersive environment. It's like you're swimming in the internet."[38]

visualization

A method of representing abstract data as images to make it easier for people to better understand the data.

In addition, researchers theorize that giving military hackers a deeper understanding of the network they are attacking will help lessen collateral damage to civilian networks. "Say we want to turn out the lights in some place where we have boots on the ground, but it's on a subnet connected to a hospital," Pound says. "We want to war-game [test] that kind of situation with high assurance, to be able to tell a commander that you can use this capability in this manner and you'll have a 99.99% chance of not failing. . . . The Oculus works hand-in-hand with that war-gaming technology."[39]

A Digital Map of the Internet

Another part of Plan X is the development of a real-time digital map of the Internet that constantly updates itself, changing as cyberspace changes. The map, which would serve as a cyberspace battlefield map, would give cyberwarriors a visual representation of global cyberspace. It would show billions of network connections, known as nodes. The idea is that access to such a map will make it easier for experts to identify potential targets and determine whether a particular network has the capability to deliver a cyberattack. If an attack appears unsustainable on a given network, it would provide hackers with alternative routes.

Experts envision the map as having blinking red dots representing enemy nodes and blinking blue dots representing American nodes. Whenever adversaries make any changes to their networks, the red dots involved in the change would immediately turn yellow. The yellow dots would alert American cyberexperts that they need to identify what changes were made before launching a cyberattack against that particular target. As Kaigham Gabriel, acting director of DARPA, explains, "In a split microsecond you could have a completely different flow of information and set of nodes. The challenge and the opportunity is to create a capability where you're always getting a rapid, high-order look of what the Internet looks like—of what the cyberspace looks like at any one point in time."[40]

immersive

Digital technology that produces three-dimensional images that seem to surround the user.

Attacking Mechanical Systems with Cyberweapons

Other cybertechnology concentrates on attacking mechanical systems controlled by computers. One of the boldest and most famous of such attacks took place in 2010. It was supposedly launched by the United States in collaboration with Israel against Iran. It entailed the planting of a worm, known as Stuxnet, into

In 2010 the Stuxnet computer virus was found on the software controlling the centrifuges used by Iran's uranium enrichment program. The virus shut down roughly a fifth of the centrifuges at the Natanz nuclear facility and was found at the Bushehr site (pictured) as well.

the computer system that controlled centrifuges vital to Iran's uranium-enrichment program. The attack was twofold. First, spyware was implanted into the computer system. The spyware identified how the Iranian computer system controlled the centrifuges and identified vulnerabilities in the system. With this information in hand, cyberexperts created the Stuxnet worm. It was designed to disable programmable controllers embedded in the Iranian computers, which operated the centrifuges. This caused the centrifuges to run at speeds that broke them apart.

To do so, Stuxnet took advantage of flaws in the operating system known as zero-day flaws. Zero-day flaws are undisclosed vulnerabilities in software or in an operating system that have not been patched and therefore cannot be defended against. The worm was introduced into the Iranian computer system via an infected USB flash drive delivered by an Iranian worker.

Because the Iranian system was air gapped, which means it was not normally connected to the Internet, Stuxnet's creators

centrifuge

A device that rotates at high speed using centrifugal force to separate substances.

did not expect the worm to spread beyond the target. Nevertheless, when a technician inadvertently connected an infected laptop to the Internet, Stuxnet spread beyond the Iranian computer system, which was how it was discovered.

Stuxnet was one of the most effective cyberattacks ever on a mechanical system operated by computers. It is believed that the worm did as much damage to Iran's uranium-enrichment program as an actual physical attack could have done. However, it also opened the possibility that other groups might attempt similar cyberattacks against mechanical systems controlled by computers. Among the most vulnerable targets are navy ships. That is why the US Navy is currently working on a cyberprotection system known as RHIMES (Resilient Hull, Mechanical, and Electrical Security).

Almost all shipboard systems, including anchoring, firefighting, steering, engine control, and electric power, are controlled by networked electromechanical systems. These systems are operated by programmable controllers embedded in computers. Currently, all of the controllers in an operating system have the same core programming. This means

> **air gapped**
>
> **A computer security measure in which computers have no external connections to other computers, external devices, or the Internet.**

that a single piece of malware designed to attack that single program can compromise every controller in the system, essentially shutting down a ship. To keep this from happening, navy scientists are working on developing a way to change the programming of each controller ever so slightly, so that each is a little different but can still do its intended job. Since the controllers are all tied to the same operating system, this is not a simple task. However, once RHIMES is perfected, it would make it practically impossible for one piece of malware to be used against more than one controller. As Ryan Craven of the Office of Naval Research explains, "Functionally, all of the controllers do the same thing, but RHIMES introduces diversity via a slightly different implementation for each controller's program. In the event of a cyberattack, RHIMES makes it so that a different hack is required to exploit

each controller. The same exact exploit can't be used against more than one controller."[41]

In addition to protecting ships, RHIMES could be used to protect civilian infrastructure such as power plants from attacks on controllers that operate mechanical systems. "Vulnerabilities exist wherever computing intersects with the physical world, such as in factories, cars and aircraft, and these vulnerabilities could potentially benefit from the same techniques for cyber resilience,"[42] Craven says.

It is not known when RHIMES will be ready for use on ships. But with all of the cybertechnology in development, it is obvious that the military is serious about protecting the United States with cutting edge cybertechnology. As Secretary of Defense Ashton Carter told American troops in 2015, "The cyber battle—battlefield—it's not a matter of the future. You can see it right now. . . . We need to be ahead of the game."[43]

Source Notes

Introduction: New Technology to Meet New Challenges

1. Quoted in Max Slowik, "The US Navy's 32-Megajoule Rail Gun Is One Step Closer to Blue Water," Guns.com, April 8, 2014. www.guns.com.
2. Quoted in History.com, "Civil War Technology," www.history .com.

Chapter One: Robots to the Rescue

3. Quoted in Tom Gardner, "Rise of the Machines: Robots May Replace a Quarter of All US Combat Troops by 2030, Claims General," *Daily Mail* (London), January 27, 2014. www.daily mail.co.uk.
4. Quoted in Christopher Snyder, "How Robots Are Helping Marines Save Lives on Battlefield," Fox News, May 24, 2015. www.foxnews.com.
5. Quoted in Maryann Lawlor, "Robots Take the Heat," *Signal*, March 2005. www.afcea.org.
6. Quoted in BBC News, "Pentagon Helps Build Meshworm Reconaissance Robot," August 9, 2012. www.bbc.com.
7. Quoted in Jason Falconer, "DARPA LS3 Quadruped Plays Follow the Leader Through Mud Puddles and More," *Gizmag*, December 20, 2012. www.gizmag.com.
8. Quoted in Luis Martinez, "Four-Legged Robot Could Help Military Handle Rough Terrain," ABC News, September 11, 2012. http://abcnews.go.com.
9. Quoted in Katie Drummond, "Pentagon Project 'Avatar' Same as the Movie but with Robots Instead of Aliens," *Wired*, February 16, 2012. www.wired.com.

Chapter Two: Unmanned Aerial and Marine Vehicles

10. Quoted in Daniel L. Byman, "Why Drones Work: The Case for Washington's Weapon of Choice," Brookings Institution, July/August 2013. www.brookings.edu.
11. Quoted in Jane Mayer, "The Predator War," *New Yorker*, October 26, 2009. www.newyorker.com.
12. Quoted in *NOVA*, "Swarming Drones," PBS.org, January 17, 2013. www.pbs.org.
13. Quoted in Brad Lendon, "US Navy Could 'Swarm' Foes with Robot Boats," CNN, October 12, 2014. www.cnn.com.
14. Quoted in Lendon, "US Navy Could 'Swarm' Foes with Robot Boats."
15. Quoted in Carl Posey, "Robot Submarines Go to War. Part 2: The Navy's UAVs," *Popular Science*, March 7, 2003. www.popsci.com.
16. Quoted in Eric Hagerman, "The Present and Future of Unmanned Drone Aircraft: An Illustrated Field Guide," *Popular Science*, February 23, 2010. www.popsci.com.

Chapter Three: State-of-the-Art Weapons

17. Quoted in Eric Adams, "Supercavitating Torpedo," *Popular Science*, June 1, 2004. www.popsci.com.
18. Quoted in Agence France-Presse, "US Navy Laser Weapon to Be Deployed Aboard USS *Ponce* in 2014," World Post, April 9, 2013. www.huffingtonpost.com.
19. Quoted in Agence France-Presse, "US Navy Laser Weapon to Be Deployed Aboard USS *Ponce* in 2014."
20. Bruce W. MacDonald, *China, Space Weapons, and US Security*. New York: Council on Foreign Relations, 2008, p. 5.

Chapter Four: Ready for Action

21. Kevin Bonsor, "How the Future Force Warrior Will Work," How Stuff Works. http://science.howstuffworks.com.
22. Quoted in Mike Hanlon, "Future Warrior Suit 2020," Gizmag, January 20, 2004. www.gizmag.com/go/3062/.

23. Quoted in Peter W. Singer, "How to Be All That You Can Be: A Look at the Pentagon's Five Step Plan for Making *Iron Man* Real," Brookings Institution, May 2, 2008. www.brookings.edu.
24. Quoted in Andy Simms, "Future Warrior Concept (Set to Stun)," Free Republic, April 10, 2007. www.freerepublic.com.
25. Quoted in Singer, "How to Be All That You Can Be."
26. Quoted in Hanlon, "Future Warrior Suit 2020."
27. Quoted in Paul F. Gorman, "The Future Soldier's Load and the Mobility of the Nation," US Army Combined Armed Center. http://usacac.army.mil.
28. Quoted in Bonsor, "How the Future Force Warrior Will Work."
29. Quoted in Sharon Weinberger, "Iron Man to Batman: The Future of Soldier Suits," BBC News, January 21, 2013. www.bbc.com.

Chapter Five: Cyberwarfare

30. Quoted in Kevin McCaney, "Cyber Operations, Electronic Warfare Will Take the Point in Future Conflicts," *Defense Systems*, September/October 2015. http://downloads.realviewtechnologies.com.
31. Quoted in Michael B. Kelley and Geoffrey Ingersoll, "How the US Invited Iranian Hackers to Attack America's Banks," *Business Insider*, October 18, 2012. www.businessinsider.com.
32. Quoted in Gilad Shiloach, "ISIS Hackers Threaten 'Message to America' Cyber Attack," Vocativ, May 11, 2015. www.vocativ.com.
33. Quoted in Mark Pomerleau, "On the Battlefield, Cyber Is Just New Weapons Payload," *Defense Systems*, November 11, 2015. https://defensesystems.com.
34. Techopedia, "Cyberattack." www.techopedia.com.
35. Quoted in Michael Mimoso, "DARPA Cyber Grand Challenge Finale Set for DEF CON 2016," Threatpost, June 4, 2014. https://threatpost.com.

36. DARPA, "Seven Teams Hack Their Way to the 2016 DARPA Cyber Grand Challenge Final Competition," July 8, 2015. www.darpa.mil.
37. Quoted in DARPA, "Seven Teams Hack Their Way to the 2016 DARPA Cyber Grand Challenge Final Competition."
38. Quoted in Andy Greenberg, "DARPA Turns Oculus into a Weapon to Prepare for Cyberwar," *Wired*, May 23, 2014. www.wired.com.
39. Quoted in Greenberg, "DARPA Turns Oculus into a Weapon to Prepare for Cyberwar."
40. Quoted in Ellen Nakashima, "With Plan X, Pentagon Seeks to Spread US Military Might to Cyberspace," *Washington Post*, May 30, 2012. www.washingtonpost.com.
41. Quoted in Phys.org, "A New Defense for Navy Ships: Protection from Cyber Attacks," September 17, 2015. http://phys .org.
42. Quoted in Phys.org, "A New Defense for Navy Ships."
43. Quoted in Mark Pomerleau, "US Prepares to Take the Cyber Fight to ISIS," *Defense Systems*, December 23, 2015. https://defensesystems.com.

For Further Research

Books

Martin Dougherty, *Artillery and Missiles*. New York: Rosen Central, 2012.

Martin Dougherty, *Military Warships Up Close*. New York: Rosen Young Adults, 2016.

Robert Jackson, *Military Jets Up Close*. New York: Rosen Young Adults, 2016.

Annie Jacobsen, *The Pentagon's Brain: An Uncensored History of DARPA, America's Top-Secret Military Research Agency*. New York: Little, Brown, 2015.

Don Nardo, *In the Air: Drones*. Greensboro, NC: Reynolds, 2014.

Don Nardo, *Special Operations: Weapons*. Greensboro, NC: Reynolds, 2013.

Internet Sources

Rebecca Boyle, "Gallery: Up Close with BigDog and Other Robots of War," *Popular Science*, September 16, 2015. www.popsci.com/slideshow-bigdog-and-other-robots-war-at-darpas-wait-what-convention?image=0.

J. Michael Cole, "Five Futuristic Weapons That Could Change Warfare," *National Interest*, November 1, 2014. http://nationalinterest.org/commentary/five-futuristic-weapons-could-change-warfare-9866.

Karl Tate, "How Unmanned Drone Aircraft Work," LiveScience, June 27, 2013. www.livescience.com/37815-how-unmanned-drone-aircraft-work-infographic.html.

Kim Zetter, "An Unprecedented Look at Stuxnet, the World's

First Digital Weapon," *Wired*, November 3, 2014. www.wired
.com/2014/11/countdown-to-zero-day-stuxnet.

Websites

Army Technology Live (http://armytechnology.armylive.dodlive
.mil). *Army Technology Live* is the official blog of the US Army
Research, Development, and Engineering Command. It provides lots of information about the Army's newest technological
breakthroughs.

DARPA (www.darpa.mil). This is DARPA's official website. It offers
lots of information about DARPA projects, research, and events.

Defense Update (http://defense-update.com). Defense Update
provides global military news related to new technology. It offers
photos, articles, videos, and news briefs.

Military Technology (www.miltechmag.com). This online mag-
azine provides news, articles, and photos of the latest military
technology.

Office of Naval Research (www.onr.navy.mil). The Office of Naval Research is involved in the development of new technology. It
provides information about its work on this website.

Index

Picture Credits

About the Author

Barbara Sheen is the author of ninety-two books for young people. She lives in New Mexico with her family. In her spare time, she likes to swim, walk, garden, and cook.